BOOKS BY PHILIP LEVINE

7 Years from Somewhere (1979)

Ashes (1979)

The Names of the Lost (1976)

1933 (1974)

They Feed They Lion (1972)

Pili's Wall (1971)

Not This Pig (1968)

On the Edge (1963)

ASHES

ASHES

POEMS NEW & OLD

by

PHILIP LEVINE

ATHENEUM   NEW YORK   1979

My thanks to the editors of the following publications
in which these poems first appeared:
The American Poetry Review (On a Drawing by Flavio,
The Red Shirt); *Antaeus* (Montjuich); *The Georgia Review*
(Any Night, Everything); *Harper's* (Lost and Found, Songs);
Inquirey (Starlight); *The Iowa Review* (Ashes, Father, The Rains,
The Water's Chant); *Kayak* (The Grave of the Kitchen Mouse);
The Missouri Review (Something Has Fallen); *The New Yorker*
(Making It New, The Miracle); *The North American Review*
(Nitrate); *Poetry* (A Woman Waking); *The Missouri Review*
(I Won, You Lost).

My special thanks to George Hitchcock, whose Kayak Press
published the following poems in my book *Red Dust* (Kayak,
1971), now out-of-print, and also for first publishing so many
of these poems in his magazine *Kayak*:
Clouds, House of Silence, Noon, In the New Sun, Fist, The
End of Your Life, Where We Live Now, Red Dust, How Much
Earth, A Sleepless Night, Told, Holding On, & The Helmet.

Library of Congress Cataloging in Publication Data

Levine, Philip, 1928-
    Ashes.

    I. Title.
PS3562.E9A9 1979   811'.5'4   78-20596
ISBN 0-689-10975-X

Published in a limited edition by
GRAYWOLF PRESS, PORT TOWNSEND, WASHINGTON

This book is for Peter Everwine
we shared the red dust of this valley

CONTENTS

I

FATHER

The long lines of diesels
groan toward evening
carrying off the breath
of the living.
The face of your house
is black,
it is your face, black
and fire bombed
in the first street wars,
a black tooth planted in the earth
of Michigan
and bearing nothing,
and the earth is black,
sick on used oils.

Did you look for me in that house
behind the sofa
where I had to be?
in the basement where the shirts
yellowed on hangers?
in the bedroom
where a woman lay her face
on a locked chest?
I waited
at windows the rain streaked
and no one told me.

I found you later
face torn
from The History of Siege,
eyes turned to a public wall
and gone
before I turned back, mouth

in mine and gone.
I found you whole
toward the autumn of my 43rd year
in this chair beside
a mason jar of dried zinnias
and I turned away.

I find you
in these tears, few,
useless and here at last.

Don't come back.

CLOUDS

1

Dawn. First light tearing
at the rough tongues of the zinnias,
at the leaves of the just born.

Today it will rain. On the road
black cars are abandoned, but the clouds
ride above, their wisdom intact.

They are predictions. They never matter.
The jet fighters lift above the flat roofs,
black arrowheads trailing their future.

2

When the night comes small fires go out.
Blood runs to the heart and finds it locked.

Morning is exhaustion, tranquilizers, gasoline,
the screaming of frozen bearings,
the failures of will, the TV talking to itself.

The clouds go on eating oil, cigars,
housewives, sighing letters,
the breath of lies. In their great silent pockets
they carry off all our dead.

3

The clouds collect until there's no sky.
A boat slips its moorings and drifts
toward the open sea, turning and turning.

The moon bends to the canal and bathes
her torn lips, and the earth goes on
giving off her angers and sighs

and who knows or cares except these
breathing the first rains,
the last rivers running over iron.

4
You cut an apple in two pieces
and ate them both. In the rain
the door knocked and you dreamed it.
On bad roads the poor walked under cardboard boxes.

The houses are angry because they're watched.
A soldier wants to talk with God
but his mouth fills with lost tags.

The clouds have seen it all, in the dark
they pass over the graves of the forgotten
and they don't cry or whisper.

They should be punished every morning,
they should be bitten and boiled like spoons.

HOUSE OF SILENCE

The winter sun, golden and tired,
settles on the irregular army
of bottles. Outside the trucks
jostle toward the open road,
outside it's Saturday afternoon,
and young women in black pass by
arm in arm. This bar
is the house of silence, and we drink
to silence without raising our voices
in the old way. We drink to doors
that don't open, to the four walls
that close their eyes, hands that run,
fingers that count change, toes
that add up to ten. Suspended
as we are between our business
and our rest, we feel the sudden peace
of wine and the agony of stale bread.
Columbus sailed from here 30 years ago
and never wrote home. On Saturdays
like this the phone still rings for him.

NOON

I bend to the ground
to catch
something whispered,
urgent, drifting
across the ditches.
The heaviness of
flies stuttering
in orbit, dirt
ripening, the sweat
of eggs.
      There are
small streams
the width of a thumb
running in the villages
of sheaves, whole
eras of grain
wakening on
the stalks, a roof
that breathes over
my head.
      Behind me
the tracks creaking
like a harness,
an abandoned bicycle
that cries and cries,
a bottle of common
wine that won't
pour.
At such times
I expect the earth
to pronounce. I say,
"I've been waiting
so long."
      Up ahead
a stand of eucalyptus

guards the river,
the river moving
east, the heavy light
sifts down driving
the sparrows for
cover, and the women
bow as they slap
the life out
of sheets and pants
and worn hands.

THE MIRACLE

A man staring into the fire
sees his dead brother sleeping.

The falling flames go yellow and red
but it is him, unmistakable.

He goes to the phone and calls
his mother. Howard is asleep,

he tells her. Yes, she says,
Howard is asleep. She does not cry.

In her Los Angeles apartment
with its small color TV

humming now unobserved,
she sees Howard rocking

alone beneath the waves
of an ocean she cannot name.

Howard is asleep, she says
to the drapes drawn on the night.

That night she dreams
a house alive with flames, their

old house, and her son sleeping
peacefully in the kingdom of agony.

She wakens near morning,
the dream more real

than the clock luminous beside her
or the gray light rising slowly

above the huddled town, more real
than the groan of the first car.

She calls her son who has risen
for work and tells him,

Howard is warm and at peace.
He sees the crusted snows of March

draining the cold light of a day
already old, he sees himself

unlocking the front door of his shop,
letting the office help in, letting

Eugene and Andy, the grease men
step before him out of the snow.

When she hangs up he looks out
on the back yard, the garbage cans

collapsing like sacks of air, the fence
holding a few gray sparrows,

he looks out on the world he always sees
and thinks, it's a miracle.

Filaments of light
slant like windswept rain.
The orange seller hawks
into the sky, a man with a hat
stops below my window
and shakes his tassels.
                              Awake
in Tetuan, the room filling
with the first colors, and water running
in a tub.

*

A row of sparkling carp
iced in the new sun, odor
of first love, of childhood,
the fingers held to the nose
for hours while the clock hummed.

The fat woman in the orange smock
places tiny greens at mouth
and tail as though she remembered
or yearned instead for forests, deep floors
of needles, and the hushed breath.

*

Blue nosed cannisters
as fat as barrels silently
slipping by. "Nitro," he says.
On the roof he shows me
where Reuban lay down
to fuck-off and never woke.
"We're takin little whiffs
all the time."
                              Slivers
of glass work their way

through the canvas gloves
and burn. Lifting my black glasses
in the chemical light, I stop
to squeeze one out and the asbestos
glows like a hand in moonlight
or a face in dreams.

                    *

Pinpoints of blue
along the arms, light rushing
down across the breasts
missing the dry shadows
under them.

                        She stretches
and rises on her knees
and smiles and far down
to the sudden embroidery of curls
the belly smiles
that three times stretched slowly moonward
in a hill of child.

                    *

Sun through the cracked glass,
bartender at the cave end
peeling a hard‚boiled egg. Four
in the afternoon,
the dogs asleep, the river
must bridge seven parched flats
to Córdoba by nightfall.
It will never make it.
                        I will
never make it. Like the old man
in gray corduroy asleep

under the stilled fan, I have
no more moves,
stranded on an empty board.

*

From the high hill
behind Ford Rouge, we could see
the ore boats pulling
down river, the rail yards,
and the smoking mountain.
East, the city spreading
toward St. Clair, miles of houses,
factories, shops burning
in the still white snow.

"Share this with your brother,"
he said, and it was always winter
and a dark snow.

FIST

Iron growing in the dark,
it dreams all night long
and will not work. A flower
that hates God, a child
tearing at itself, this one
closes on nothing.

Friday, late,
Detroit Transmission. If I live
forever, the first clouded light
of dawn will flood me
in the cold streams
north of Pontiac.

It opens and is no longer.
Bud of anger, kinked
tendril of my life, here
in the forged morning
fill with anything—water,
light, blood—but fill.

First light. This misted field
   is the world, that man
      slipping the greased bolt

back and forth, that man
   tunneled with blood
      the dark smudges of whose eyes

call for sleep, calls
   for quiet, and the woman
      down your line,

the woman who screamed the loudest,
   will be quiet.
      The rushes, the grassless shale,

the dust, whiten like droppings.
   One blue
      grape hyacinth whistles

in the thin and birdless air
   without breath.
      Ten minutes later

a lost dog poked
   for rabbits, the stones
      slipped, a single blade

of grass stiffened in sun;
   where the wall
      broke a twisted fig

thrust its arms ahead
    like a man
       in full light blinded.

In the full light the field
    your eyes held
       became grain by grain

the slope of father mountain,
    one stone of earth
       set in the perfect blackness.

THE RAINS

The river rises
and the rains keep coming.
My Papa says
it can't flood for
the water can run
away as fast as
it comes down. I believe
him because he's Papa
and because I'm afraid
of water I know I can't stop.
All day in school I
see the windows darken,
and hearing the steady drum
of rain, I wonder
if it will ever stop
and how can I get home.

It did not flood.
I cannot now remember
how I got home.
I recall only that the house
was dark and cold, and I went
from room to room calling
out the names
of all those I lived with
and no one answered. For a time
I thought the waters had swept
them out to sea
and this was all I had. At last
I heard the door opening
downstairs and my brother
stamping his wet boots
on the mat.

Now when the autumn comes
I go alone

into the high mountains
or sometimes with my wife,
and we walk in silence
down the trails
of pine needles
and hear the winds
humming through the branches
the long dirge of the world.
Below us is the world
we cannot see, have come
not to see, soured
with years of never
giving enough, darkened
with oils and fire, the world
we could have come
to call home.

One day the rain
will find us far
from anything, crossing
the great meadows
the sun had hidden in.
Hand in hand, we
will go forward toward nothing
while our clothes darken
and our faces stream
with the sweet waters
of heaven. Your eyes,
suddenly deep and dark in that light,
will overflow with joy
or sadness, with all
you have no names for.
This is who you are.
That other life below
was what you dreamed
and I am the man beside you.

WHERE WE LIVE NOW

1

We live here because the houses
are clean, the lawns run
right to the street

and the streets run away.
No one walks here.
No one wakens at night or dies.

The cars sit open-eyed
in the driveways.
The lights are on all day.

2

At home forever, she has removed
her long foreign names
that stained her face like hair.

She smiles at you, and you think
tears will start from the corners
of her mouth. Such a look

of tenderness, you look away.
She's your sister. Quietly she says,
You're a shit, I'll get you for it.

3

Money's the same, he says.
He brings it home in white slabs
that smell like soap.

Throws them down
on the table as though
he didn't care.

The children hear
and come in from play glowing
like honey and so hungry.

4
With it all we have
such a talent for laughing.
We can laugh at anything.

And we forget no one.
She listens to mother
on the phone, and he remembers

the exact phrasing of a child's sorrows,
the oaths taken by bear and tiger
never to forgive.

5
On Sunday we're having a party.
The children are taken away
in a black Dodge, their faces erased

from the mirrors. Outside a scum
is forming on the afternoon.
A car parks but no one gets out.

Brother is loading the fridge.
Sister is polishing and spraying herself.
Today we're having a party.

6
For fun we talk about you.
Everything's better for being said.
That's a rule.

This is going to be some long night, she says.
How could you? How could you?
For the love of mother, he says.

There will be no dawn
until the laughing stops. Even the pines
are burning in the dark.

7
Why do you love me? he says.
Because. Because.
You're best to me, she purrs.

In the kitchen, in the closets,
behind the doors, above the toilets,
the calendars are eating it up.

One blackened one watches you
like another window. Why
are you listening? it says.

8
No one says, There's a war.
No one says, Children are burning.
No one says, Bizniz as usual.

But you have to take it all back.
You have to hunt through your socks
and dirty underwear

and crush each word. If you're serious
you have to sit in the corner
and eat ten new dollars. Eat 'em.

9
Whose rifles are brooding
in the closet? What are
the bolts whispering

back and forth? And the pyramids
of ammunition, so many
hungry mouths to feed.

When you hide in bed
the revolver under the pillow
smiles and shows its teeth.

10

On the last night the children
waken from the same dream
of leaves burning.

Two girls in the dark
knowing there are no wolves
or bad men in the room.

Only electricity on the loose,
the television screaming at itself,
the dishwasher tearing its heart out.

11

We're going away. The house
is too warm. We disconnect
the telephone.

Bones, cans, broken dolls, bronzed shoes,
ground down to face powder. Burn
the toilet paper collected in the basement.

Take back the bottles.
The back stairs are raining glass.
Cancel the milk.

12

You may go now, says Cupboard.
I won't talk,
says Clock.

Your bag is black and waiting.
How can you leave your house?
The stove hunches its shoulders,

the kitchen table stares at the sky.
You're heaving yourself out in the snow
groping toward the front door.

This harpie with dry red curls
talked openly of her husband,
his impotence, his death, the death
of her lover, the birth and death
of her own beauty. She stared
into the mirror next to
our table littered with the wreck
of her appetite and groaned:
Look what you've done to me!
as though only that moment
she'd discovered her own face.
Look, and she shoved the burden
of her ruin on the waiter.

I do not believe in sorrow;
it is not American.
At 8,000 feet the towns
of this blond valley smoke
like the thin pipes of the Chinese,
and I go higher where the air
is clean, thin, and the underside
of light is clearer than the light.
Above the tree line the pines
crowd below like moments of the past
and on above the snow line
the cold underside of my arm,
the half in shadow, sweats with fear
as though it lay along the edge
of revelation.

And so my mind closes around
a square oil can crushed on the road
one morning, startled it was not

the usual cat. If a crow
had come out of the air to choose
its entrails could I have laughed?
If eagles formed now in the
shocked vegetation of my sight
would they be friendly? I can hear
their wings lifting them down, the feathers
tipped with red dust, that dust which
even here I taste, having eaten it
all these years.

HOW MUCH EARTH

Torn into light, you woke wriggling
on a woman's palm. Halved, quartered,
shredded to the wind, you were the life
that thrilled along the underbelly
of a stone. Stilled in the frozen pond
you rinsed heaven with a sigh.

How much earth is a man.
A wall lies down and roses
rush from its teeth; in the fists
of the hungry, cucumbers sleep
their lives away, under your nails
the ocean moans in its bed.

How much earth.
The great ice fields slip
and the broken veins of an eye
startle under light, a hand is planted
and the grave blooms upward
in sunlight and walks the roads.

A SLEEPLESS NIGHT

April, and the last of the plum blossoms
scatters on the black grass
before dawn. The sycamore, the lime,
the struck pine inhale
the first pale hints of sky.
                              An iron day,
I think, yet it will come
dazzling, the light
rise from the belly of leaves and pour
burning from the cups
of poppies.
                    The mockingbird squawks
from his perch, fidgets,
and settles back. The snail, awake
for good, trembles from his shell
and sets sail for China. My hand dances
in the memory of a million vanished stars.

A man has every place to lay his head.

TOLD

The air lay softly on the green fur
of the almond, it was April

and I said, I begin again
but my hands burned in the damp earth

the light ran between my fingers
a black light like no other

this was not home, the linnet
settling on the oleander

the green pod swelling
the leaf slowly untwisting

the slashed egg fallen from the nest
the tongue of grass tasting

I was being told by a pulse slowing
in the eyes

the dove mourning in shadow
a nerve waking in the groin

the distant hills
turning their white heads away

told by the clouds assembling
in the trees, told by the blooming

of a black mouth beneath the rose
the worm sobbing, the dust

settling on my eyelid, told
by salt, by water, told and told.

The last of day gathers
in the yellow parlor
and drifts like fine dust
across the face of
the gilt-framed mirror
I often prayed to.
An old man's room
without him, a room I
came back to again
and again to steal
cigarettes and loose change,
to open cans of sardines,
to break open crackers
and share what he had.
Something is missing.
The cut glass ashtray
is here and overflowing,
the big bottle of homemade,
the pack of English Ovals,
the new red bicycle deck
wrapped in cellophane
and gold edged, the dishes
crusted with the last snack.
The music is gone. The lilt
of his worn voice broken
with the weight of all
those lost languages—
"If you knew Solly like
I knew Solly, oy oy
oy what a girl." That music
made new each day and absent
forever from the corners

of rooms like this one
darkening with dusk.
The music a boy would laugh
at until it went out
and days began and ended
without the banging fist,
without the old truths
of blood and water, without
the loud cries of *I won*,
you lost, without song.

ANY NIGHT

Look, the eucalyptus, the Atlas pine,
the yellowing ash, all the trees
are gone, and I was older than
all of them. I am older than the moon,
than the stars that fill my plate,
than the unseen planets that huddle
together here at the end of a year
no one wanted. A year more than a year,
in which the sparrows learned
to fly backwards into eternity.
Their brothers and sisters saw this
and refuse to build nests. Before
the week is over they will all
have gone, and the chorus of love
that filled my yard and spilled
into my kitchen each evening
will be gone. I will have to learn
to sing in the voices of pure joy
and pure pain. I will have to forget
my name, my childhood, the years
under the cold dominion of the clock
so that this voice, torn and cracked,
can reach the low hills that shielded
the orange trees once. I will stand
on the back porch as the cold
drifts in, and sing, not for joy,
not for love, not even to be heard.
I will sing so that the darkness
can take hold and whatever
is left, the fallen fruit, the last
leaf, the puzzled squirrel, the child
far from home, lost, will believe
this could be any night. That boy,
walking alone, thinking of nothing
or reciting his favorite names

to the moon and stars, let him
find the home he left this morning,
let him hear a prayer out
of the raging mouth of the wind.
Let him repeat that prayer,
the prayer that night follows day,
that life follows death, that in time
we find our lives. Don't let him see
all that has gone. Let him love
the darkness. Look, he's running
and singing too. He could be happy.

II

STARLIGHT

My father stands in the warm evening
on the porch of my first house.
I am four years old and growing tired.
I see his head among the stars,
the glow of his cigarette, redder
than the summer moon riding
low over the old neighborhood. We
are alone, and he asks me if I am happy.
"Are you happy?" I cannot answer.
I do not really understand the word,
and the voice, my father's voice, is not
his voice, but somehow thick and choked,
a voice I have not heard before, but
heard often since. He bends and passes
a thumb beneath each of my eyes.
The cigarette is gone, but I can smell
the tiredness that hangs on his breath.
He has found nothing, and he smiles
and holds my head with both his hands.
Then he lifts me to his shoulder,
and now I too am there among the stars,
as tall as he. Are you happy? I say.
He nods in answer, Yes! oh yes! oh yes!
And in that new voice he says nothing,
holding my head tight against his head,
his eyes closed up against the starlight,
as though those tiny blinking eyes
of light might find a tall, gaunt child
holding his child against the promises
of autumn, until the boy slept
never to waken in that world again.

A WOMAN WAKING

She wakens early remembering
her father rising in the dark
lighting the stove with a match
scraped on the floor. Then measuring
water for coffee, and later the smell
coming through. She would hear
him drying spoons, dropping
them one by one in the drawer.
Then he was on the stairs
going for the milk. So soon
he would be at her door
to wake her gently, he thought,
with a hand at her nape, shaking
to and fro, smelling of gasoline
and whispering. Then he left.
Now she shakes her head, shakes
him away and will not rise.
There is fog at the window
and thickening the high branches
of the sycamores. She thinks
of her own kitchen, the dishwasher
yawning open, the dripping carton
left on the counter. Her boys
have gone off steaming like sheep.
Were they here last night?
Where do they live? she wonders,
with whom? Are they home?
In her yard the young plum tree,
barely taller than she, drops
its first yellow leaf. She listens
and hears nothing. If she rose
and walked barefoot on the wood floor

no one would come to lead her
back to bed or give her
a glass of water. If she
boiled an egg it would darken
before her eyes. The sky tires
and turns away without a word.
The pillow beside hers is cold,
the old odor of soap is there.
Her hands are cold. What time is it?

EVERYTHING

Lately the wind burns
the last leaves and evening
comes too late to be
of use, lately I learned
that the year has turned
its face to winter
and nothing I say or do
can change anything.
So I sleep late and waken
long after the sun has risen
in an empty house and walk
the dusty halls or sit
and listen to the wind
creak in the eaves and struts
of this old house. I say
tomorrow will be different
but I know it won't.
I know the days are shortening
and when the sun pools
at my feet I can reach
into that magic circle
and not be burned. So
I take the few things
that matter, my book,
my glasses, my father's ring,
my brush, and put them aside
in a brown sack and wait—
someone is coming for me.
A voice I've never heard
will speak my name
or a face press to the window
as mine once pressed
when the world held me out.
I had to see what it was

it loved so much. Nothing
had time to show me
how a leaf spun itself
from water or water cried
itself to sleep for
every human thirst. Now
I must wait and be still
and say nothing I don't know,
nothing I haven't lived
over and over,
and that's everything.

Green fingers
holding the hillside,
mustard whipping in
the sea winds, one blood-bright
poppy breathing in
and out. The odor
of Spanish earth comes
up to me, yellowed
with my own piss.
                              40 miles from Málaga
half the world away
from home, I am home and
nowhere, a man who envies
grass.
                    Two oxen browse
yoked together in the green clearing
below. Their bells cough. When
the darkness and the wet roll in
at dusk they gather
their great slow bodies toward
the stalls.
                         If my spirit
descended now, it would be
a lost gull flaring against
a deepening hillside, or an angel
who cries too easily, or a single
glass of seawater, no longer blue
or mysterious, and still salty.

SONGS

Dawn coming in over the fields
of darkness takes me by surprise
and I look up from my solitary road
pleased not to be alone, the birds
now choiring from the orange groves
huddling to the low hills. But sorry
that this night has ended, a night
in which you spoke of how little love
we seemed to have known and all of it
going from one of us to the other.
You could tell the words took me
by surprise, as they often will, and you
grew shy and held me away for a while,
your eyes enormous in the darkness,
almost as large as your hunger
to see and be seen over and over.

30 years ago I heard a woman sing
of the motherless child sometimes
she felt like. In a white dress
this black woman with a gardenia
in her hair leaned on the piano
and stared out into the breathing darkness
of unknown men and women needing
her songs. There were those among
us who cried, those who rejoiced
that she was back before us for a time,
a time not to be much longer, for
the voice was going and the habits
slowly becoming all there was of her.

And I believe that night she cared
for the purity of the songs and not
much else. Oh, she still saw
the slow gathering of that red dusk
that hovered over her cities, and no

doubt dawns like this one caught
her on the roads from job to job,
but the words she'd lived by were
drained of mystery as this sky
is now, and there was no more "Easy
Living" and she was "Miss Brown" to
no one and no one was her "Lover Man."
The only songs that mattered were wordless
like those rising in confusion from
the trees or wind-songs that waken
the grass that slept a century, that
waken me to how far we've come.

MONTJUICH

"Hill of Jews," says one,
named for a cemetery
long gone."Hill of Jove,"
says another, and maybe
Jove stalked here
once or rests now
where so many lie
who felt God swell
the earth and burn
along the edges
of their breath.
Almost seventy years
since a troop of cavalry
jingled up the silent road,
dismounted, and loaded
their rifles to deliver
the fusillade into
the small, soft body
of Ferrer, who would
not beg God's help.
Later, two carpenters
came, carrying his pine
coffin on their heads,
two men out of movies
not yet made, and near dark
the body was unchained
and fell a last time
onto the stones.
Four soldiers carried
the box, sweating
and resting by turns,
to where the fresh hole
waited, and the world
went back to sleep.
The sea, still dark

as a blind eye,
grumbles at dusk,
the air deepens and a chill
suddenly runs along
my back. I have come
foolishly bearing red roses
for all those whose blood
spotted the cold floors
of these cells. If I
could give a measure
of my own for each
endless moment of pain,
well, what good
would that do? You
are asleep, brothers
and sisters, and maybe
that was all the God
of this old hill could
give you. It wasn't
he who filled your
lungs with the power
to raise your voices
against stone, steel,
animal, against
the pain exploding
in your own skulls,
against the unbreakable
walls of the State.
No, not he. That
was the gift only
the dying could hand
from one of you
to the other, a gift
like these roses I fling

off into the night.
You chose no God
but each other, head,
belly, groin, heart, you
chose the lonely road
back down these hills
empty handed, breath
steaming in the cold
March night, or worse,
the wrong roads
that led to black earth
and the broken seed
of your body. The sea
spreads below, still
as dark and heavy
as oil. As I
descend step by step
a wind picks up and hums
through the low trees
along the way, like
the heavens' last groan
or a song being born.

NITRATE

They don't come back, he said.
Outside it was dinnertime,
and Granpa's wagon swayed
at the curb, the old gray
shaking his head from side to side
like he wanted to lie down
where the snows had burned off
and dark patches of ground shone.
The house was quiet
so Granpa told me everything
and I understood. They went in
but they never came out.
The hole in the earth
was what they called The Mines,
and that's where his little brother
went in to make his food.
There were horses too
burning up with their carts
like Granpa's bottle cart.
The walls were white as sugar,
soft, and the roots of trees
spun in your face. Granpa wiped
his forehead with the wool cap
and sat staring at the blue smoke
curling from his mouth and said
it was all for a dollar.
He didn't like to cry.
He bowed his head down
and hid his face in his hands,
so he never saw our favorite
Chinese elm out in the front yard,
the green leaves hissing

and steaming like kettles.
A new spring was here
in the last slanting light,
the wren nest went up
in a moment of gold, the eggs
darkening like knuckles.
When the tree was gone
all that was left
was a little mound of salt.

All morning
rain slowly filled
my hair, misted
my glasses as I broke
the old curbing of u s 24,
and Cal, grunting behind,
loaded the pieces
into the wheelbarrow.
"Go slow, man!" but I
was into it. Now, at noon,
we sit under a tree
sharing my lunch. Cal
looks tired, his light
brown skin almost gray.
His father, he tells me,
caught him last night
with white boys in his room.
"I told him, 'Don't look
and you won't see.'" The rain
comes down harder, a wind
picks up, swirling
the few leaves crushed
under the trees. My damp arms
shiver in the sudden chill
of autumn. We are the dignified
by dirt, digging our way
down u s 24 to Monroe,
Michigan, where the waters
of Raisin Creek foam
with the milk poured
from the mill, and the great
slow barges from Nineveh
drift in the current,
loaded with yellow spices,
rubies like headlights,

and the whores of the East.
Cal lies back and closes
his eyes. I smoke and let
him sleep. An hour passes
and not one car. At first
his blanket of newspaper
rises in the breeze, a giant
butterfly mottled with slaps
of rain. Cal sleeps on,
his face as open and soft
as a child's, his feet
crossed at the ankles,
the black leather cap
fallen back on the grass.
"Cal," he said the first day,
staring into my eyes,
"is short for Calla, the lily,"
the yellow furled one
his mother so loved. Far off
a car hisses down the road;
it's Teddy, the Captain, come
to tell us it's raining
and we can fly home
or go back to work
or get lost. I leave
Cal, the dark wet bride
of the wind, and go
out into the rain
to get the word—we aren't
ever gonna make Monroe.

THE RED SHIRT

" . . . his poems that no one
reads anymore become 'dust,
wind, nothing,' like the in-
solent colored shirt he bought
to die in." VARGAS LLOSA

If I gave 5 birds
each 4 eyes
I would be blind
unto the 3rd
generation, if I
gave no one a word
for a day
and let the day
grow into a week
and the week sleep
until it was
half of my life
could I come home
to my father
one dark night?

On Sundays an odd light
grows on the bed
where I have lived
this half of my life
a light that begins
with the eyes
blinding first one
and then both
until at last
even the worn candles
in the flower box
lay down their heads.

Therefore I have come
to this red shirt
with its faultless row
of dark buttons, 7
by my count, as dark
as blood that poured
over my lips
when the first word
of hope jumped
and became a cry
of birds calling
for their wings,
a cry of new birds.

This is the red shirt
Adam gave to the Angel
of Death when he asked
for a son, this
is the flag Moses
waved 5 times
above his head
as he stumbled
down the waves
of the mountainous sea
bearing the Tables of 10,
this is the small cloth
mother put in
my lunch box
with bread and water.

This is my red shirt
in which I go to meet
you, Father of the Sea,
in which I will say
the poem I learned

from the mice. A row
of faultless buttons,
each one 10 years
and the eye of the bird
that beheld the first world
and the last, a field
of great rocks weeping,
and no one to see
me alone, day after
day, in my red shirt.

THE HELMET

All the way
on the road to Gary
he could see
where the sky shone
just out of reach
and smell the rich
smell of work
as strong as money,
but when he got there
the night was over.

People were going
to work and back,
the sidewalks were lakes
no one walked on,
the diners were saying
time to eat
so he stopped
and talked to a woman
who'd been up late
making helmets.

There are white hands
the color of steel,
they have put their lives
into steel,
and if hands could lay down
their lives these hands
would be helmets.
He and the woman
did not lie down

not because
she would praise
the steel helmet

boarding a train
for no war,
not because
he would find
the unjewelled crown
in a surplus store
where hands were sold.

They did not lie down
face to face
because of the waste
of being so close
and they were too tired
of being each other
to try to be lovers
and because they had
to sit up straight
so they could eat.

Above my desk
the Rabbi of Auschwitz
bows his head and prays
for us all, and the earth
which long ago inhaled
his last flames turns
its face toward the light.
Outside the low trees
take the first gray shapes.
At the cost of such
death must I enter
this body again,
this body which is
itself closing on
death? Now the sun
rises above a stunning
valley, and the orchards
thrust their burning
branches into the day.
Do as you please, says
the sun without uttering
a word. But I can't.
I am this hand that
would raise itself
against the earth
and I am the earth too.
I look again and closer
at the Rabbi and at last
see he has my face
that opened its eyes
so many years ago

to death. He has these
long tapering fingers
that long ago reached
for our father's hand
long gone to dirt, these
fingers that hold
hand to forearm,
forearm to hand because
that is all that God
gave us to hold.

SOMETHING HAS FALLEN

Something has fallen wordlessly
and holds still on the black driveway.

You find it, like a jewel,
among the empty bottles and cans

where the dogs toppled the garbage.
You pick it up, not sure

if it is stone or wood
or some new plastic made

to replace them both.
When you raise your sunglasses

to see exactly what you have
you see it is only a shadow

that has darkened your fingers,
a black ink or oil,

and your hand suddenly smells
of classrooms when the rain

pounded the windows and you
shuddered thinking of the cold

and the walk back to an empty house.
You smell all of your childhood,

the damp bed you struggled from
to dress in half-light and go out

into a world that never tired.
Later, your hand thickened and flat

slid out of a rubber glove,
as you stood, your mask raised,

to light a cigarette and rest
while the acid tanks that were

yours to clean went on bathing
the arteries of broken sinks.

Remember, you were afraid
of the great hissing jugs.

There were stories of burnings,
of flesh shredded to lace.

On other nights men spoke
of rats as big as dogs.

Women spoke of men
who trapped them in corners.

Always there was grease that hid
the faces of worn faucets, grease

that had to be eaten one
finger-print at a time,

there was oil, paint, blood,
your own blood sliding across

your nose and running over
your lips with that bright, certain

taste that was neither earth
or air, and there was air,

the darkest element of all,
falling all night

into the bruised river
you slept beside, falling

into the glass of water
you filled two times for breakfast

and the eyes you turned upward
to see what time it was.

Air that stained everything
with its millions of small deaths,

that turned all five fingers
to grease or black ink or ashes.

THE GRAVE OF
THE KITCHEN MOUSE

The stone says "Coors"
The gay carpet says "Camels"
Spears of dried grass
The little sticks the children gathered
The leaves the wind gathered

The cat did not kill him
The dog did not, not the trap
Or lightning, or the rain's anger
The tree's claws
The black teeth of the moon
The sun drilled over and over

Dusk of his first death
The earth is worn away
A tuft of gray fur ruffles the wind
One paw, like a carrot
Lunges downward in darkness
For the soul

Dawn scratching at the windows
Counted and closed
The doors holding
The house quiet
The kitchen bites its tongue
And makes bread

THE WATER'S CHANT

Seven years ago I went into
the High Sierras stunned by the desire
to die. For hours I stared into a clear
mountain stream that fell down
over speckled rocks, and then I
closed my eyes and prayed that when
I opened them I would be gone
and somewhere a purple and golden
thistle would overflow with light.
I had not prayed since I was a child
and at first I felt foolish saying
the name of God, and then it became
another word. All the while
I could hear the water's chant
below my voice. At last I opened
my eyes to the same place, my hands
cupped and I drank long from
the stream, and then turned for home
not even stopping to find the thistle
that blazed by my path.
                              Since then
I have gone home to the city
of my birth and found it gone,
a gray and treeless one now in its place.
The one house I loved the most
simply missing in a row of houses,
the park where I napped on summer days
fenced and locked, the great shop
where we forged, a plane of rubble,
the old hurt faces turned away.
My brother was with me, thickened
by the years, but still my brother,
and when we embraced I felt the rough
cheek and his hand upon my back tapping

as though to tell me, I know! I know!
brother, I know!
                    Here in California
a new day begins. Full dull clouds ride
in from the sea, and this dry valley
calls out for rain. My brother has
risen hours ago and hobbled to the shower
and gone out into the city of death
to trade his life for nothing because
this is the world. I could pray now,
but not to die, for that will come one
day or another. I could pray for
his bad leg or my son John whose luck
is rotten, or for four new teeth, but
instead I watch my eucalyptus,
the giant in my front yard, bucking
and swaying in the wind and hear its
tidal roar. In the strange new light
the leaves overflow purple and gold,
and a fiery dust showers into the day.

ASHES

Far off, from the burned fields
of cotton, smoke rises and scatters
on the last winds of afternoon.
The workers have come in hours ago,
and nothing stirs. The old bus creaked
by full of faces wide-eyed with hunger.
I sat wondering how long the earth
would let the same children die day
after day, let the same women curse
their precious hours, the same men bow
to earn our scraps. I only asked.
And now the answer batters the sky:
with fire there is smoke, and after, ashes.
You can howl your name into the wind
and it will blow it into dust, you
can pledge your single life, the earth
will eat it all, the way you eat
an apple, meat, skin, core, seeds.
Soon the darkness will fall on all
the tired bodies of those who have
torn our living from the silent earth,
and they can sleep and dream of sleep
without end, but before first light
bloodies the sky opening in the east
they will have risen one by one
and dressed in clothes still hot
and damp. Before I waken they are
already bruised by the first hours
of the new sun. The same men
who were never boys, the same women
their faces gone gray with anger,
and the children who will say nothing.
Do you want the earth to be heaven?
Then pray, go down on your knees

as though a king stood before you,
and pray to become all you'll
never be, a drop of sea water,
a small hurtling flame across the sky,
a fine flake of dust that moves
at evening like smoke at great height
above the earth and sees it all.

A light wind beyond the window,
and the trees swimming
in the golden morning air.
Last night for hours I thought
of a boy lost in a huge city,
a boy in search of someone
lost and not returning. I thought
how long it takes to believe
the simplest facts of our lives—
that certain losses are final,
death is one, childhood another.
It was dark and the house creaked
as though we'd set sail for
a port beyond the darkness.
I must have dozed in my chair
and wakened to see the dim shapes
of orange tree and fig against
a sky turned gray, and a few
doves were moaning from the garden.
The night that seemed so final
had ended, and this dawn becoming
day was changing moment
by moment—for now there
was blue above, and the tall grass
was streaked and blowing, the quail
barked from their hidden nests.
Why give up anything? Someone
is always coming home, turning
a final corner to behold the house
that had grown huge in absence
now dull and shrunken, but the place
where he had come of age, still
dear and like no other. I have
come home from being lost,

home to a name I could accept,
a face that saw all I saw
and broke in a dark room against
a wall that heard all my secrets
and gave nothing back. Now he
is home, the one I searched for.
He is beside me as he always
was, a light spirit that brings
me luck and listens when I speak.
The day is here, and it will last
forever or until the sun fails
and the birds are once again
hidden and moaning, but for now
the lost are found. The sun
has cleared the trees, the wind
risen, and we, father and child
hand in hand, the living and
the dead, are entering the world.

PHILIP LEVINE was born in 1928 in Detroit and was formally educated there, at the public schools and at Wayne State University. After a succession of stupid jobs he left the city for good, living in various parts of the country before he settled in Fresno, California, where he now teaches. His books include *On the Edge* (1963), *Not This Pig* (1968), *Pili's Wall* (1971), *They Feed They Lion* (1972), *1933* (1974), *The Names of the Lost* (1976) and *7 Years from Somewhere* (1979).